World War 2

*A Captivating Guide from
Beginning to End*

Contents

Free Bonus from Captivating History (Available for a Limited time)

Hi History Lovers!

Now you have a chance to join our exclusive history list so you can get your first history ebook for free as well as discounts and a potential to get more history books for free! Simply visit the link below to join.

Captivatinghistory.com/ebook

Also, make sure to follow us on:

Twitter: @Captivhistory

Facebook: Captivating History: @captivatinghistory

Introduction

The Second World War was one of the most traumatic events in human history. Across the world, existing conflicts became connected, entangling nations in a vast web of violence. It was fought on land, sea, and air, touching every inhabited continent. Over 55 million people died, some of them combatants, some civilians caught up in the violence, and some murdered by their own governments.

It was the war that unleashed the Holocaust and the atomic bomb upon the world. But it was also a war that featured acts of courage and self-sacrifice on every side.

The world would never be the same again.

Chapter 1 – The Rising Tide

The Second World War grew out of conflicts in two parts of the world: Europe and East Asia. Though the two would eventually become entangled, it's easier to understand the causes of the war by looking at them separately.

Europe's problems were rooted in centuries of competition between powerful nations crammed together on a small and densely populated continent. Most of the world's toughest, most stubborn, and most ambitious kids were crammed together in a single small playground. Conflict was all but inevitable.

The most recent large European conflict had been the First World War. This was the first industrialized war, a hugely traumatic event for all the participants. In the aftermath, Germany was severely punished for its aggression by the victorious Allied powers. The remains of the Austro-Hungarian empire fell apart, creating instability in the east. And the Russian Empire, whose government had been overthrown during the turmoil of the war, became the Union of Soviet Socialist Republics (USSR), the first global power to adopt the new ideology of communism.

From this situation of instability, a new form of politics emerged. Across Europe, extreme right-wing parties adopted ultra-nationalistic views. Many of them incorporated ideas of racial superiority. Most were strongly influenced by the fear of communism. All relied on scapegoating outsiders to make themselves more powerful.

The first to reach prominence was the Fascist Party in Italy under Benito Mussolini. Mussolini was a veteran soldier, gifted orator, and skilled administrator. He rallied disenchanted left-wingers and those who felt put down by corrupt politicians and forceful trade unions. Using a mixture of persuasion and intimidation, he won the 1922 election and became prime minister. Through a series of laws, he turned his country into a one-party dictatorship. Most of his achievements were domestic, bringing order and efficiency at the price of freedom, but he also had ambitions abroad. He wanted Italy to be a colonial power like Britain or France, and so in 1935-6 his forces conquered Abyssinia.

Mussolini was surpassed in almost every way by the man who reached power in Germany a decade later—Adolph Hitler. A decorated veteran of the First World War, Hitler was embittered at the Versailles Treaty, which imposed crushing restrictions upon Germany in the aftermath of the war. He developed a monstrous ideology that combined racism, homophobia, and a bitter hatred of communism. Like Mussolini, he brought together oratory and street violence to seize control of Germany. Once elected chancellor in 1933, he purged all opposition and had himself made Führer, the nation's "leader" or "guide." He then escalated the rearmament of Germany, casting off the shackles of Versailles.

Hitler and Mussolini intervened in the Spanish Civil War of 1936-9. Rather than have their nations join the war, they sent parts of their armed forces to support Franco's right-wing armies, testing new military technology and tactics while ensuring the victory of a man they expected to be an ally—a man who would in fact keep his nation out of the coming war for Europe.

Meanwhile, Hitler was playing a game of chicken with the other European powers. In March 1936, he occupied the Rhineland, a part of Germany that had been demilitarized after the war. Two years later, he annexed his own homeland of Austria, with its large German-speaking population. He occupied parts of Czechoslovakia that fall and finished the job off the following spring. At every turn, the rest of Europe backed down rather than go to war to protect less powerful nations.

Meanwhile, in Asia, the Chinese revolutions of 1911 and 1913, along with the Chinese Civil War that broke out in 1927, had triggered a parallel period of instability. Nationalists and communists battled for control of a vast nation, destroying the regional balance of power.

Japan was a nation on the rise. Economic growth had created a sense of ambition which had then been threatened by a downturn in the 1930s. Interventions by Western powers, including their colonies in Asia and a restrictive naval treaty of 1930, embittered many in Japan, who saw the Europeans and Americans as colonialist outsiders meddling in their part of the world.

The Japanese began a period of expansion, looking to increase their political dominance and their control of valuable raw resources. They invaded Chinese Manchuria in 1931 and from then on kept encroaching on Chinese territory. At last, in 1937, the Chinese nationalist leader Chiang Kai-Shek gave up on his previous policy of giving ground to buy himself time. A minor skirmish escalated into the Second Sino-Japanese War.

From an Asian point of view, the war had already begun. But it would be Hitler who pushed Europe over the brink and gave the war its Western start date of 1939.

Chapter 2 – From Poland to the Fall of France

Hitler had long looked at Poland with hungry eyes. He believed in the racial superiority of Germans and wanted more space for them to live in. Poland, just over the border to the east, was perfect. Many Nazi supporters had fought against Polish incursions following the First World War, and so they were already primed for conflict with the Poles.

On September 1, 1939, German troops swept across the Polish border. It was a war the Germans had long been preparing for. Under the secret terms of the Molotov-Ribbentrop Pact, Germany and the USSR had agreed not only to keep the peace between themselves but to partition Poland between them. Meanwhile, German forces had been gathering on the Polish border.

Fifty-five German divisions swept into Poland. These were primarily tanks and motorized infantry, allowing them to advance swiftly. The Luftwaffe, the German air force, pounded the Polish defenses. With only 17 divisions at the front and 22 more preparing, the Poles were vastly outnumbered. It was the same in the air, where 4,700 modern German planes faced the 842 outdated aircraft of the Polish air force. On top of this, some German troops were already experienced soldiers, veterans of the fighting in Spain.

This was the first example of what came to be called Blitzkrieg—"lightning war." German commanders such as Heinz Guderian had long been advocating such a fast-paced, hard-hitting form of warfare. The open plains of Poland were the perfect place to showcase what they could do.

The Germans advanced 140 miles in the first week, reaching the borders of Warsaw. There, at the Polish capital, some of the fiercest fighting took place.

On September 17, the Russians invaded Poland from the east. Most of the Polish forces had already been smashed by the Germans. The following day, the Polish high command fled into exile. Eighty thousand soldiers followed them, fleeing to France and Britain. The Warsaw garrison surrendered on September 28, the last substantial Polish forces on October 5.

The Poles had powerful allies. They had had a treaty with France since 1921 and one with Britain since 1939. On September 3, Britain and France declared war on Germany. Australia, Canada, New Zealand, and South Africa, all independent dominions within the British Commonwealth, followed their parent country's lead. But none of them were close enough to help as Poland was engulfed.

The months that followed are often referred to as the "phony war" due to the lack of direct conflict between the major belligerents. But this hides the frantic activity going on across Europe.

While the invasion of Poland was still underway, the French made a brief and half-hearted attempt to invade the German Saarland, only to run up against the carefully prepared defenses of the Siegfried Line.

In the east, the USSR began swallowing up territory not yet occupied by the Germans. This included a grueling invasion of Finland, known as the Winter War, in which poorly prepared Soviet troops became bogged down in bitter cold that stopped vehicles from working and froze men to death. Though the Russians gained territory from the Finns, it was in many ways a Pyrrhic victory.

The Allies began a naval blockade of Germany. The power of the British Royal Navy gave them a huge advantage.

The Germans countered with submarines, known as U-boats, which slipped out into the Atlantic to attack convoys bringing vital war supplies to Britain and France. These supplies included equipment hastily ordered from the Americans, who were happy to play a profitable part in bolstering friendly nations without entangling themselves in a European war.

Meanwhile, Polish troops arrived in Britain and France. They brought with them cryptographers who had begun work on breaking the Enigma code, used for Germany's highest-level military communications. This fed into the work of British military intelligence, which in a matter of months was turned from a neglected corner of government into the world's leading organization for covert information gathering and analysis.

In April 1940, Germany invaded Denmark and Norway to protect shipping routes for vital iron ore from Sweden. British, French, and Polish troops rushed to support the Norwegians. But once again, the Germans swiftly overwhelmed their opponents.

One important result of the failure in Norway was a change of government in Britain. On May 10, 1940, Winston Churchill replaced Neville Chamberlain as prime minister. Churchill, long a belligerent and divisive figure in British politics, formed a coalition government that united the country for war. His strong leadership would prove vital in the days ahead.

Just as Churchill was taking up his new role, Germany was preparing for its most dramatic success of the war—the invasion of France. As forces gathered on the western border over the winter, the German army had adopted a revised plan of action developed by Field Marshal Erich von Manstein. Manstein's plan shifted the focus of the German offensive south, so that the main strike would come through the Ardennes forest, a region supposedly impassable to a modern army. That change of plan proved critical.

One hundred and thirty-six German army divisions had been gathered for the invasion. Facing them were 94 French, 22 Belgian, and 10 British divisions. The Germans had fewer tanks than their opponents, but the superior quality of those tanks and the skill of tank commanders such as Guderian and Erwin Rommel would give the Germans the advantage in armored forces.

On May 10, 1940, the Germans launched their attack.

In the Netherlands, the Dutch army was swiftly overwhelmed by the forces of their more powerful neighbor. The Dutch surrendered after only four days of fighting.

In Belgium, the attack began with the arrival of German paratroopers on the roof of the massive concrete fort at Eben Emael, part of a defensive system along the Albert Canal. The paratroopers destroyed the gun turrets and defeated a garrison that outnumbered them more than ten to one. With the Belgian defensive line weakened, its armies outnumbered, and half the air force quickly destroyed, the nation was swiftly overrun with German troops.

At the southern end of the advance, German Panzer divisions—fast-moving units consisting of tanks and their supporting troops—raced through the Ardennes in southern Belgium and burst into France. The French had not been prepared for an attack in this area and so the Germans hit them at the point where two of their weakest armies joined. The Germans quickly broke through, fought their way across the River Meuse, and then raced northwest. On May 20, they reached the English Channel, splitting the Allied forces in half.

The British Expeditionary Force, along with French and other Allied troops, were surrounded on a shrinking patch of ground. On May 26, the British began evacuating these beleaguered troops through the port of Dunkirk, while a French rearguard held off the Germans; 338,000 men, including 120,000 French, were evacuated. Their survival was vital to maintaining the Allied war effort and helped to boost morale back in Britain, but some in France saw this as a betrayal, abandoning them in their hour of need.

With the Channel coast clear, the Germans swept south, surrounding the bulk of the remaining French troops. Many of the French were stationed on the Maginot Line, a system of concrete fortresses that the Germans had simply bypassed with their Ardennes offensive. Once again, the French were outmaneuvered and overwhelmed.

The French, militarily beaten, surrendered on June 22. The country was divided. The north and west were occupied by the Germans. The southeast became a puppet state under the right-wing Vichy regime.

Meanwhile, on June 10, Mussolini sent troops across the Alps into southeastern France. It was a token effort to claim some glory and territory before Hitler got it all. More importantly, it brought Italy into the war.

Chapter 3 – Britain's Darkest Hour

The months that followed have achieved near-legendary status in Britain, and not without reason. Half of Europe had been overrun by the Axis powers of Germany and Italy. The nations that hadn't been conquered, including Sweden, Ireland, and Spain, remained neutral. Of the sovereign states of Europe, only Britain stood against an alliance of aggressive regimes.

As is so often the case, the truth is far less simple than the legend, and the British were never really alone.

In Britain, the armed forces were suddenly bolstered by a wave of refugees—soldiers, airmen, and seamen who had survived the fall of their countries and come to fight with Britain against a mutual enemy. The French brought substantial forces led by General de Gaulle. Evacuees from Poland included airmen, soldiers, and the vital specialists who had been researching the Enigma code.

Further afield, Britain was supported by the remains of its empire and by the Commonwealth, a collection of ex-imperial nations. Of the most prominent imperial and Commonwealth states, Australia and India would both contribute to the war in Asia, while Canadians would play a vital and often costly part in later European campaigns. More immediately, these nations kept Britain supplied with the resources it needed to fight on.

Within Europe, resistance networks were emerging to fight the Nazis. British covert operatives were smuggled onto the continent to provide them with arms and organizational help, but their acts of resistance, which included intelligence gathering, sabotage, and the assassination of Nazi officials, were carried out by local partisans risking death at the hands of a murderous regime.

From December 1940, America also began to play a more important part in the war. In a radio address to the nation, President Franklin D. Roosevelt set out his intention for America to become the "arsenal of democracy," providing the Allies in Europe with the military equipment they needed to fight against Germany and Italy. Roosevelt had to walk a delicate line. While he favored intervention in the war, many Americans preferred to maintain a policy of neutrality. The policy of arming free Europe, and to a lesser extent China, was a way of holding back imperial powers without committing America to a war it was not yet willing to fight.

One result of Roosevelt's decision was a rise in the importance of the Atlantic convoys. These merchant fleets, protected by military ships, were a vital lifeline for the British. They brought in not only war material manufactured in the United States but also a large part of the raw materials Britain needed to feed and arm itself. In 1941 alone, Britain imported 6.4 million metric tons of iron, steel, and iron ore, 13.1 million tons of oil, and 5.4 million tons of wheat. All of this despite the German submarines prowling the seas.

The successes of the Atlantic convoys, like so many other British successes in the war, were built in part upon ever-evolving intelligence work. Techniques in cryptography, aerial reconnaissance, human intelligence gathering, and analysis of the results took huge leaps forward. The cracking of the Enigma code, though important, was only one part in this great machine. Entire teams were dedicated to identifying and tracking German submarines. German advances in rocketry were followed. With the help of resistance operatives in Norway, the feared German battleship *Bismarck* was run to ground and sunk. Every single German spy in Britain was either imprisoned or turned into a double agent in the opening months of the war.

Meanwhile, Hitler was making plans to invade Britain. Operation Sealion would involve 43 German divisions crossing the Channel, surrounding London, and forcing the surrender of the British government.

This was no idle whim. Tanks were waterproofed and fitted with snorkels ready for amphibious landings. Artillery batteries were lined up along the French coast ready to bombard Britain. Ships and men were assembled.

As these preparations were underway, it became increasingly clear that Germany would need aerial superiority if it was to successfully cross the Channel. The German navy couldn't even clear mines without coming under attack from the Royal Air Force (RAF). Given the number of transport ships available, the Germans would have to cross in more than one wave, increasing their exposure to the RAF during that crossing.

So the Luftwaffe set out to gain control of the skies above Britain. Starting on August 8, 1940, hundreds of aircraft were launched every day to bomb British radar stations and airfields.

Around 1,300 German bombers and dive bombers were deployed in the Battle of Britain, along with 1,200 fighters to protect them. The RAF had around 600 fighters capable of front-line duty, most of them Hurricanes and Spitfires. Though most RAF pilots were British, some came from occupied countries. Four whole squadrons were manned by Poles and one by Czechs.

The Germans were confident, thanks to their superior numbers. But technologically, the Allies were at an advantage. At this stage in the war, their planes were generally better than those of the Germans, which included the Messerschmitt Bf 110 "destroyer," known by many as "Goering's folly" for its flawed design. The British also had a complete radar network covering their southern and eastern coastline, the most advanced radar network in the world. This let them see the Germans coming, get planes into the air to face them, and then direct those planes onto their targets.

For the first few months, the Germans focused on military installations. They attacked airbases, then ports and airfields, then radar stations, looking for the best way to cripple the RAF. Allied pilots were exhausted from constant combat, the RAF fighting on the edge of collapse.

All of this changed in August. On the 24th, a German plane accidentally dropped its bombs on civilian buildings in London. Prime Minister Winston Churchill ordered a retaliatory strike, and the next night British bombers hit Berlin. Hitler, who had promised his people that this would not happen, was furious. He shifted the Luftwaffe's focus off military targets and onto cities. Their aim was now to smash British industry and shred the enemy's morale through terror bombing.

Hundreds of tons of bombs fell nightly on London and other cities. The carnage was terrible, but it gave the RAF the rest they needed as attacks on their bases stopped. In mid-September, the balance of the fighting shifted. Now the Allies were destroying enemy planes faster than the Germans could make them. It became clear that the Germans were not going to win.

The bombing continued, but the risk of invasion looked vanishingly small.

While the air war hung in the balance, Operation Sealion was repeatedly postponed. Worsening weather made a cross-Channel invasion impossible until the spring. By the time better weather came around, Hitler had fixed his eyes on a new target.

Britain had survived its darkest hour.

Chapter 4 – Barbarossa Unleashed

In the years following the First World War, Germany and the USSR had had relatively cordial relations. The Soviets, alongside the Swedes, had helped the Germans to rebuild their military strength, in contravention of the terms of the Treaty of Versailles. German forces had even taken part in training operations in Russia, during which some of the lessons that led to Blitzkrieg were learned. In 1939, the Molotov-Ribbentrop Pact saw these two powerful nations agree to divide eastern Europe into separate spheres of influence and to maintain a state of non-aggression.

None of this meant anything to Hitler, despite his part in forging the pact. Communism was one of the hate figures upon which he had fixed, a bogey man that he considered a threat to the human spirit and to the new order he was building. He wanted to conquer the USSR to provide Germans with more living space, to further his agenda of wiping out Communists and Jews, and to increase Germany's strategic power through the land and raw resources this conquest would provide.

In December 1940, he signed a directive setting out his intention to "crush Soviet Russia in one rapid campaign." He believed that, just like in Poland and France, German forces could overwhelm the enemy, conquering the USSR in three months through a blitzkrieg strike. The plan was titled Operation Barbarossa.

British and American intelligence learned in advance about Hitler's plan. In hopes of goading the Soviet leader, Josef Stalin, into acting against Hitler, they told him what they knew. But Stalin believed that Hitler would stand by the Molotov-Ribbentrop Pact. After all, the USSR was a great power and Germany already faced enemies to the west.

Over three million German soldiers, divided into 152 divisions, were mustered ready for the operation. Once again, the spearhead of the attack would be motorized forces, in the form of 17 panzer and 13 motorized infantry divisions. Nearly 2,000 Luftwaffe planes would support the advance.

Germany also brought in allies.

In 1940, following the partition of Poland, the USSR had occupied parts of Romania. Romania responded by allying itself with Germany and Italy. The Romanians sent 14 divisions to join Barbarossa, wanting an opportunity to take back their lost land.

The Finns were in a similar position, having lost territory to the Soviets during the Winter War. They supplied 17 divisions.

At 0530 on June 22, 1941, the German ambassador in Moscow delivered a declaration of war, claiming that the Soviets had violated the terms of the non-aggression pact. Axis troops started advancing across a 1,900-mile long border that ran from the Black Sea to the Baltic.

In the early weeks of the operation, the Germans had the advantage. The Soviets had 150 divisions on the frontier and more coming to their aid, making them nearly a match in numbers. But the Germans were better trained and equipped. They had experience from fighting in Poland, Norway, Belgium, and France. While the Russians had more tanks and planes, the German ones were better. And while the Soviets had some capable commanders, they had also lost many to Stalin's purges, leaving the Germans at an advantage in experienced and skilled leadership.

Though only 20% of their troops were equipped for the lightning advance of Blitzkrieg, the Germans made swift advances. By the end of July, they swallowed up a stretch of the USSR twice as large as France. They surrounded entire Soviet armies and forced them to give up, including

600,000 soldiers at Minsk and Smolensk and another 665,000 at Kiev. They arrived in time to take in most of Ukraine's summer harvest, providing the Germans with food and just as critically taking it away from the Soviets. This happened despite Stalin's orders that, as when Napoleon had invaded 120 years before, the Russians should scorch the earth as they withdrew, depriving the invaders of supplies.

Food wasn't the only thing that the Germans were harvesting. The SS, the Nazi party's ideologically driven stormtroopers, made up a significant part of the advancing armies. Hitler had planned the campaign with their activities in mind. They immediately began murdering people the Nazis had singled out as inferior or objectionable: commissars, responsible for spreading and upholding communist ideology; Slavs, the majority population of parts of the USSR, who the Nazis considered degenerate; Jews, the most prominent scapegoats of Hitler's regime. At Baby Yar, 100,000 Ukrainian Jews were marched into a ravine north of the city and killed.

The brutality of the German occupation wasted one of the advantages they went in with—resentment at the Soviet regime. In the Baltic states, parts of Belorussia and areas of the Ukraine, they were initially welcomed as an alternative to Russian occupation or communist dictatorship. It is a cruel irony that the Jews of Kiev at first welcomed the Germans, who had treated them well during the First World War. But the murderous agenda of the Nazi party ensured that the new arrivals were soon seen as just more cruel invaders.

Based on the first few weeks, the Nazi commanders considered the invasion a huge success. They were driving the Soviets before them and wiping their opponents off the map. But bit by bit, the German advance slowed down. Two hundred more divisions of Soviet troops arrived, allowing Stalin to counter German training and technology with weight of numbers. Hitler's personal interventions led to some indecisive action on the part of the Germans, as the Führer switched between plans. A delay outside Leningrad allowed the Soviets to dig in there, beginning a siege that would last until 1944 and kill over 800,000 civilians. On the approach to Leningrad, the Finns halted their part of the war. They had retaken their lost territory and didn't want to invite future Soviet aggression by invading part of the USSR.

The power of Russian industry came into play. By the fall of Vyazma and Bryansk in October, they had only 824 tanks left on the front and no air support. But they had the capacity to rebuild. Stalin had built up an armaments industry based on quantity and uniformity, as opposed to the quality and variety that the Germans prized. This industrial machine could churn out massive numbers of tanks, planes, and supporting vehicles based on tractor designs. The USSR's population of farmers, who had been driving those same tractors for years, provided a ready pool of vehicle operatives, while millions of ordinary peasants were conscripted into an army of staggering scale.

To focus on quantity isn't to say that the Soviet equipment was necessarily bad. The T-34 tank, which the Germans faced in growing numbers, was perhaps the best tank of the war. It forced the Germans to develop new vehicles of their own. And the Russians kept churning them out. To keep production going, Stalin moved entire factories east, away from the German threat.

America and Britain played their part by providing materials for Russia's war effort. The British were eager to see the Axis occupied on another front, while the Americans saw this as an extension of the arsenal of democracy.

Then came the same force that had saved Russia from Napoleon in 1812—the winter. It was the coldest Russian winter for 140 years. Tanks became immobile as the oil froze in their engines. Artillery shells were stuck together as the grease they were packed in froze. Trenches could not be dug because of frozen ground. Frostbite hit the German soldiers, whose uniforms were not warm enough for such terrible conditions.

As the latest advance on Moscow ground to a halt, the German army faced its opponents across a land of ice and snow.

Chapter 5 – Early Operations in Africa and the Mediterranean

Like Hitler, Mussolini had eyes on an eastern prize. While the Führer prepared for his war against the Soviet behemoth, his Italian ally was launching an offensive against a more vulnerable target in the form of Greece. This, together with Italian operations in North Africa, opened up the Mediterranean as a major theatre of war.

Italy's Mediterranean operations began while the Battle of France was still ongoing. In June 1940, they began a siege of the island of Malta, a relatively small target but one that was strategically important because of its position on supply routes through the Mediterranean. British and Commonwealth forces there held out against aerial bombing and naval blockades for the next two years.

After conquering British Somaliland in August, the Italians then began invasions of British-held Egypt in September and of Greece in October.

The Italians invaded Greece through Albania, which they had occupied just before the outbreak of the war. It was a campaign which was meant to prove that they were just as powerful as their German allies.

It ended up having the exact opposite effect. Seven Italian divisions were held up by a small force of Greeks, who drove them back out of the country and then went on the offensive. By the middle of December 1940, the Italians had lost a third of Albania. Meanwhile, the British and their Commonwealth allies offered the Greeks support, sending troops in to defend the country. This alarmed the Germans, as it put the Allies close to the Romanian oil fields, whose resources the German war machine desperately needed.

In North Africa, the Italians had colonial territory in Libya. To the east was Egypt, protected by British and Commonwealth troops, who were there to support the Egyptians and defend the Suez Canal, a vital transport route connecting the Mediterranean to the Indian Ocean. In mid-September 1940, the Italians crossed the border and advanced 50 miles into Egypt, occupying British bases.

The British and Indians countered in early December. Operation Compass, a five-day raid, drove the Italians out of Egypt. With Australian reinforcements, the British and Indians went on the attack, making decisive advances into Libya. They took the port of Tobruk, drove their opponents back 500 miles, and took 130,000 prisoners before the Italian 10th Army surrendered on February 7.

Meanwhile, the British Royal Navy had attacked the Italian fleet in harbor at Taranto. The Italians lost half their capital ships to a raid by torpedo bombers, severely hindering their ability to fight at sea.

By early 1941, things were looking bad for the Italians. They had been defeated and embarrassed on nearly every front. Hitler, fearful for the consequences if this continued, decided to step in. It was a move that would avert military disaster but do little to restore lost Italian dignity.

That spring, the German Afrika Corps arrived in Libya. It was led by General Rommel, one of the men who had led the German panzer divisions to such success in France. Rommel went on the offensive in March, driving the Allies back as far as the Egyptian border. They held on in Tobruk, which fell under siege by Axis forces for months. For the rest of the year, the war went back and forth, both sides experiencing a mixture of successes and defeats. The Allies were eventually able to relieve Tobruk and claim some victories, but Rommel had proven himself a challenging foe.

In March 1941, Bulgaria and Yugoslavia made alliances with the Axis powers. The Yugoslavian government was almost immediately overthrown by a British-backed coup. And so, in April, the Germans used their access to the region through Bulgaria to launch invasions of both Greece and Yugoslavia. Germany's fast-moving and powerful way of making war once again triumphed and both nations were conquered within a month.

British and Commonwealth forces retreated to the Greek island of Crete, allowing them to keep a foothold in the Balkans. But this didn't last. On May 20, the Germans launched the invasion of Crete, one of the most spectacular airborne operations in history. Paratroopers and glider-borne infantry swept across the island, overwhelming local partisans and Commonwealth forces. Despite some hard fighting, in which the soldiers of New Zealand played a prominent part, the Allies were forced to evacuate by the beginning of June.

For the major powers, the Balkans became a backwater of the war. But Yugoslavia remained a thorn in the German side throughout, as hard-fighting partisan forces launched persistent guerilla operations from hidden bases in the hills.

Further east, challenges in the Middle East threatened the British eastern flank in Egypt. Syria and Lebanon were controlled by Vichy French forces. In April 1941, a coup put a pro-Axis government in charge of Iraq.

The British and Commonwealth troops responded with a swift campaign to regain control of Iraq, where they had military bases before the war. Having installed a puppet government favorable to them, they moved on to invade the Vichy-held territories and so shore up their position in North Africa. This time they were assisted by Free French forces. The Vichy troops put up strong resistance, but the whole campaign was still over in less than a month, ending in victory for the Allies.

In Africa, the strategies of both sides were dictated in large part by supply lines. It was hard to support extended lines across the desert and so the British withdrew a little in January 1942.

Rommel responded by going on the offensive. In a series of attacks, he pushed the Allied forces back. In June, he beat them at the Battle of Gazala. Tobruk was surrounded and surrendered to Axis forces in June, as the Allies could no longer supply the port for an extended siege.

In July, the Allies drove off a series of German attacks in the First Battle of El Alamein, halting Rommel's advance. He attacked again at the end of August, but was defeated by the British under their new commander, General Bernard Montgomery, at the Battle of Alam el Halfa. This had been Rommel's last chance to overrun Egypt before more troops arrived to bolster the Allies. From now on, the tide of war would turn against him.

Montgomery's presence also played a part in turning the tide of war. In October, he led the British and Commonwealth troops in a fresh offensive, defeating Rommel at the Second Battle of El Alamein.

Rommel began a steady retreat east. This was done despite orders from Hitler, who commanded him to hold his ground. This became a recurring theme as the war turned against Germany. Hitler would order his commanders to fight on no matter what, not surrendering territory to the enemy. They, realizing the need for tactical retreats, would face the choice between challenging their leader, disobeying him, or carrying out orders they knew to be futile.

Rommel pulled back east while Montgomery steadily advanced. The German commander sometimes sacrificed his infantry to preserve his more valuable armored forces. By the end of 1942, they were halfway across Libya and heading for Tunisia, another Axis-controlled territory. But

by then the whole shape of the war had changed.
The Americans were coming.

Chapter 6 – A Day Which Will Live in Infamy

While war raged in Europe and North Africa, Japanese actions in East Asia were setting in motion the events that would turn this into a global war.

In September 1940, Japan signed a treaty with Germany and Italy, bringing it into the alliance known as the Axis. Though Japan was not committed to fighting at their side, it was showing where its allegiances lay.

Meanwhile, the war in China raged on. The American government provided support to Chiang Kai-Shek and the nationalist forces resisting the Japanese invasion, as well as imposing sanctions on Japan. American troops might not be there on the ground, but it was another intervention by Western powers against a nation that already resented their presence.

Hitler's successes in Europe forced the Japanese government's hand. They wanted to take control of the European colonies in Asia. If they waited too long and the Germans seized control of Europe, Hitler's government would then lay claim to the colonies of the nations they had conquered. Japan needed to deal with China and grab those colonies before it was too late.

In November 1941, the Japanese sent the US an ultimatum, demanding that it lift its embargo, stop supporting the Chinese, and start selling the Japanese the oil they needed to power their war machine. The Americans were just as cornered diplomatically as the Japanese. If they gave in then Britain would lose the raw resources of its empire, the Axis would dominate in Europe, and the USA would be faced on all sides by hostile powers. So America refused to accede to the demands.

On December 7, 1941, Japan launched a surprise attack on the American naval base at Pearl Harbor in the Hawaiian Islands. It was primarily an air attack, using bombers launched from Japanese aircraft carriers, though submarines were also involved.

Devastating as the attack was, it did not achieve its goal. The American aircraft carriers were not in port and so these vital resources were not hit by the attack.

This was not the only attack launched by the Japanese that day. They also invaded Hong Kong, Guam, Wake Island, Midway, and the Philippines, where a large American force fought a fighting retreat before being cut off and forced to surrender. The Japanese were making a huge grab for power.

Though negotiations had been increasingly tense over the previous month, the Americans considered the Pearl Harbor attack to be a great break from diplomatic protocol, as it was not preceded by a declaration of war. President Roosevelt labeled December 7 as "a day which will live in infamy." The American public was outraged. The following day, the government declared war against Japan, with only a single congressman voting against the declaration. Isolationism, so long the bedrock of American foreign policy, had been decisively smashed.

Britain joined the Americans in declaring war on Japan. British territory was being invaded and Britain and the Commonwealth had the resources to play a meaningful part in the war, despite commitments in Europe and Africa.

Over the following days, Japan continued to occupy small territories around its sphere of influence. On December 10, Japanese forces sank the HMS *Prince of Wales* and the HMS *Repulse*, the two most powerful British warships in the region. The Japanese were riding high on a wave of success.

The relationship between Germany and Japan was not a close one. When the Germans declared war on the USSR, Japan declined to join them. Though Japan and the Soviets were rivals who had fought in the past, the Japanese were happy to see their opponents distracted and saw no need to join in. But on December 11, Hitler came out in support of Japan by declaring war on the US. It was a move that ensured that America would commit to the war in Europe, not just Asia. America responded by declaring war on Germany and Italy.

The diplomatic fallout from Pearl Harbor turned separate conflicts in Europe and Asia into a single war that circled the globe.

America quickly began gearing up for war. Young men rushed to join the armed forces. Boatloads of freshly recruited marines began journeys across the Pacific, the ships taking winding routes to avoid Japanese submarines. Both sides knew that aircraft carriers would be critical to the conflict and so many naval pilots also had to be recruited. The military industry expanded to produce vast quantities of munitions, weapons, vehicles, and other supplies.

One of Japan's most important objectives was to take Australia. As part of the Commonwealth, the Australians were a major source of troops for the British. They were also friendly trading partners with America. Australia would provide a southern anchor to island territories scattered across the western Pacific.

The Japanese worked their way south toward Australia, swallowing territory as they went. The East Indies, Guam, and Wake Island all became part of their empire. Soon, they would have the bases they needed to cut off supply lines between Australia and the USA.

The first major battle between Japanese and Allied forces took place in May 1942. An American fleet, with some

Australian support, took on the Japanese in a battle of great historical significance. For the first time ever, two fleets fought without their ships even seeing each other. The engagement was decided entirely by air power, as planes from aircraft carriers attacked the opposing fleets.

The Battle of the Coral Sea was not a decisive encounter. The Japanese did more damage than the Allies but suffered losses that would hamper them in the next fleet battle. Strategically, it was the first time that a Japanese advance had been halted. In that sense, it was an important symbolic moment.

The more militarily decisive moment came a month later. A Japanese fleet was heading toward Midway Island, which was defended by American aircraft and ground forces. If the Japanese took Midway, they could use it as a base from which to launch attacks on Pearl Harbor, threatening America's ability to act in the western Pacific.

As the Japanese approached Midway, they were attacked by planes from the island and from an American fleet coming up behind them. Though the Japanese pilots in their Zero fighters performed well, it was not enough to win. They lost four aircraft carriers, which the Japanese could ill afford to replace, while the Americans, who were already working on more ships, lost only one carrier. The invasion force was turned back and the Americans gained a decisive advantage at sea. The tide of war was about to turn.

While this was going on, another front opened up that would see Japanese ground forces in constant conflict with the Allies for the rest of the war. In December 1941, the Japanese and their Thai allies invaded Burma, a part of the British Empire. There, they drove back British forces, including those from imperial India, and Chinese troops. They were initially very successful, occupying most of Burma. But it was a success that would stall, creating a fighting front that would last for the rest of the war.

Chapter 7 – Germany's Eastern Offensives

In Europe, most fighting was still taking place on the Eastern front, where German military faced the massive industrial and human resources of the Soviet Union.

One of the greatest mistakes Hitler made was underestimating how much material, both human and industrial, Stalin could bring to the war. Without even the distraction of war with Japan, he could draw in the military resources of the eastern provinces of the USSR. Even as fresh materials were being made and new soldiers recruited, existing troops were flowing west ready to face the invaders.

The first serious Soviet counter-offensive took place in the winter of 1941-2. The Germans had been held up outside Moscow. Now was the time to drive them back and remove the threat to the Soviet capital.

The offensive began on December 5. The Soviets had only a slight edge over the Germans in numbers, but by careful deployment they were able to outnumber them two to one at significant points along the front.

The offensive progressed slowly at first but built up some momentum. Solnechnogorsk and Klin were recaptured. The Germans were forced into a retreat.

German commanders wanted to make tactical withdrawals to save their forces, but Hitler would not let them. Arguments behind the scenes saw upheaval in the senior ranks of the army and men disobeying orders. After much disruption, limited withdrawals were finally allowed.

The Soviets tried several times to surround and destroy parts of the invading force. The German Third Panzer Army and then the Second Panzer Army both escaped such traps. XXXIX Corps was surrounded and destroyed while buying time for others to retreat.

With freezing weather interfering with German planes, the Soviets matched their opponents in the skies for the first time. But the Luftwaffe still helped to keep the German army alive, providing air cover as troops pulled back.

After a month of progress, the Soviet offensive ran out of steam. The battle lines settled down. Soviet troops had driven the Germans back for the first time. Moscow looked far safer than it had a month before.

The Soviets launched another counter-attack in the spring. This time, it ended in disaster. Two Siberian divisions were encircled by the Germans outside Leningrad. A tank force punched through the Romanian Sixth Army, only to be surrounded by the Germans. Six hundred tanks and a quarter of a million men fell into Axis hands.

As the weather improved, the Germans prepared to launch a fresh offensive. Called Case Blue, this time their plan was focused not on the Soviet heartland but on the Baku oil fields in the south. This would provide the Germans with vital supplies of fuel, depriving the Soviets of the same resources. It would also threaten British India.

Case Blue was a two-pronged offensive. Army Group A advanced across the Caucasus Mountains and into the oil fields. To their north, Army Group B protected their flank through an advance toward the city of Stalingrad.

The offensive began in late June. Army Group A made slow progress toward its goal. Many of the troops being used were not suited to mountain warfare. The further they progressed, the more problems arose with getting supplies to them, due to the logistical challenges of long supply lines in difficult terrain. Progress toward the oil fields ground to a halt.

When it became clear that the Germans were not going to take the oil fields for themselves, Hitler decided on another option. If they couldn't have the oil then they could at least stop the Soviets from using it. The Luftwaffe began a bombing campaign aimed at destroying the oil infrastructure. But again, the Germans fell short of their goals. They could only reach some of the refineries by direct routes, meaning that the Soviets could tell where the bombers would be coming. As more Soviet planes reached the region and the Germans had to draw some of theirs off to fight elsewhere, it became clear that the oil fields were not going to be taken out. The Germans had hampered the Soviets' ability to fuel themselves but not struck the decisive blow they had hoped for.

Army Group B began its main advance in late July, heading toward the River Don. In most places, they were able to push the Soviets back across the river, but some bridgeheads remained, threatening the Axis forces.

On August 23, the Germans crossed the Don, establishing their own bridgehead on the far side. On the same day, German forces reached the outskirts of Stalingrad, beginning one of the most bitterly fought battles of the war. After the Soviet 62nd Army was almost encircled by German forces, the Soviets retreated elsewhere on the front. Stalingrad become the focal point of the whole offensive.

The Battle of Stalingrad was one of the bloodiest in the history of war. Nearly two million people were killed, wounded, or captured in the fighting. It was the ruin of German ambitions in Russia.

For the first three months, Axis forces were on the offensive. While other Axis troops, including Romanians and Hungarians, guarded their flanks, the Germans launched a devastating assault on the city. Artillery and bombers pounded away while troops advanced through the ruined streets.

Here, the Germans could not use the fast-flowing blitzkrieg tactics that had stood them in good stead elsewhere. They became bogged down in street fighting, to which the Soviets swiftly adjusted. Though Axis forces continued to make progress for three months, capturing most of the city west of the Volga, it cost them dearly. Russian soldiers held out in isolated pockets long after the Germans had passed by, meaning that nowhere was secure. Nowhere felt safe. One German veteran said that "The streets are no longer measured in meters, but in corpses."

On November 19, the Soviets launched a counter-attack. Rather than face the Germans in the city head on, they attacked to the north and south. They punched through the weaker Axis forces holding the flanks and surrounded the German army.

The roles had been reversed and now the Germans were the ones under siege. As a Soviet offensive drove Axis forces back elsewhere and those at Stalingrad tightened their grip, the German Sixth Army became increasingly isolated and short of supplies. As was his way, Hitler would not allow them to surrender despite the desperate circumstances. They had no hope of winning. At last, on February 2, 1943, the last German forces in Stalingrad were defeated. The mighty Sixth Army had been lost, along with all its veteran troops.

Soviet confidence received a massive boost, while German morale plummeted. As the Germans and their allies were pushed back, the Kursk Salient developed—a bulge in the lines near Kursk, in which Soviet troops had pushed back the Germans. The Germans responded by developing their last great offensive on the Eastern Front—Operation Citadel.

The fundamental point of Citadel was simple. Axis forces would advance from north and south into the neck of the Kursk Salient, joining up to cut off the Soviet troops there.

It would allow them to destroy a significant part of the Soviet armed forces and retake the offensive.

But the Soviets had also been making plans, preparing counter-offensives for just such an occasion. Warned about the German plans by British intelligence, they prepared a defense in depth for the salient.

In July 1943, the Germans launched their operation, triggering a fresh period of intense fighting. The war in the Mediterranean meant that they did not have all the resources the commanders hoped for, but they still thought that there was a chance for victory.

The Battle of Kursk is best remembered for large tank clashes, including the Battle of Prokhorovka, one of the largest tank battles in history. Up and down the lines, the Soviets held up the German attacks, robbing them of the decisive victory that they needed. After a week and a half, the German offensive ended, to be replaced by Soviet offensives. It became clear that the Germans would not achieve what Hitler wanted and Citadel was called off. It was a victory for the Soviets.

Stalingrad was the turning point on the Eastern Front, but Kursk ended German hopes for another reversal. The invasion begun with Operation Barbarossa had turned into a grinding mess which was eating up German resources in a series of failed offensives. Things were about to get even worse for Hitler's armies, as the Russians gained the initiative and went on the attack.

Chapter 8 – Guadalcanal and the War in Asia

The Germans weren't the only Axis power losing the initiative in the war. In the Pacific, the tide of Japanese expansion was about to be halted and then reversed as the Allies went on the offensive.

The Allied offensive began on New Guinea, a large island territory to the north of Australia. It had several advantages as a starting point. It would be easy to support troops there, thanks to the proximity of the Allied fleets. It would also be easy to move in supplies, given how close it was to the Australian mainland. And the Japanese had already been halted there.

The Japanese had originally landed in New Guinea on the north side of the island. A guerilla campaign had contained them there in the area around Salamaua. An invasion force had been prepared to land at Port Moresby, on the south side of the island, giving the Japanese overall control. But this fleet was halted by the lack of a clear Japanese victory in the Battle of the Coral Sea. Meanwhile, Australian troops, supported by a smaller force of Americans, were assembling on the south side of the island.

July and August 1942 saw clashes between the Allies and newly arrived Japanese troops. Australian forces conducted a fighting retreat, during which they gained valuable experience of jungle fighting. Extended supply lines and Allied air attacks hampered the Japanese advance. Finally, in late September, the Allies began their own offensive.

Over the next year, they launched a series of successful attacks against the Japanese. Time and again, the Allies inflicted far heavier casualties than they received. Through a combination of cross-country marches and amphibious landings, they repeatedly isolated Japanese troops, forcing them to retreat or hold out in tiny enclaves. As the Japanese lost their supply lines and troops sent to reinforce them were lost at sea, their situation became increasingly desperate.

But while the Japanese never regained the initiative, they never gave up; 13,500 Japanese soldiers held on in New Guinea until they surrendered at the end of the war.

Meanwhile, the Americans began their main campaign with the battle that made the name of the US Marine Corps.

Guadalcanal was a British possession in the Solomon Islands. In July 1942, Japanese troops landed there and began building an airstrip. To prevent the Japanese gaining a base for air power in the region, the Americans hastily threw together an invasion force of Marines.

They landed on August 7 and took the airfield the next day, giving them a base of operations. The Japanese had withdrawn into the jungle rather than face the full weight of the invasion force. The Marines hurriedly finished work on the airfield so that their own planes could land.

Control of the seas around Guadalcanal was vital. The Japanese at first had the naval advantage, letting them bombard the American ground troops using planes and naval guns. For three months, the Americans and Australians could not risk sending in ships to support the Marines.

In November, the Allies finally got a naval victory, sinking two Japanese battleships. They took control of the waters around Guadalcanal, ensuring that they received the supplies they needed and that the Japanese were deprived of theirs.

On the island, the Marines had dug in around the airfield, from which an air group gave them the best support it could with limited resources. The Americans saw for the first time how the Japanese fought, including the unsettling banzai charges, hundreds of men racing fearlessly at the enemy gun lines. The fighting was often fierce, the Japanese launching desperate charges that ended in heavy casualties and sometimes brutal hand-to-hand combat, men killing each other up close.

One of the darkest elements of the fighting was the behavior of wounded Japanese soldiers. Rather than surrender to the Americans, they would often lie quietly until the victors came to check on them, then make suicidal attacks. As a result, American soldiers started shooting or stabbing corpses rather than risk them turning out to still be alive and ready to attack. The Japanese unwillingness to accept the dishonor of capture or defeat was changing their opponents as well as them.

The horrors of Guadalcanal weren't just about the fighting. Dysentery and malaria took their toll, as did shortages of supplies and sleep, night watches and shore bombardments robbing men of their rest.

But the same problems faced the Japanese, who were having no luck driving back the Americans. Their government finally grew weary of their losses. In February, they secretly withdrew their troops from the island, leaving it to the Americans.

While Guadalcanal was the most important and protracted fight the Americans were engaged in, it wasn't the only one. In February 1943, they landed on the Russell Islands. A campaign of air attacks in the Aleutians from August 1942 led to an invasion in May 1943, in which they seized control of the islands, putting them within bombing range of Japan. A series of operations in and around New Britain led to the isolation of the large Japanese force at Rabaul, letting the Allies bypass this army rather than having to take it on.

Meanwhile, the fight for Burma continued. The British, including imperial troops from India, tried to hold out against Japanese aggression and even go on the offensive. But they weren't prepared for much of what the Japanese threw at them, including offensives through supposedly impassable jungle that turned the Allied flank. Two small Allied offensives during the dry season proved ineffective and they were forced to withdraw toward the Indian border.

One of the problems the British faced was the state of India. This was their most solid base in the region and it was becoming increasingly unstable. Famine in Bengal added to already growing resentment of British rule. Troops had to be committed to keeping the peace, reducing the forces that could be sent into Burma.

In the jungles and steep hills of Burma, the British developed new ways of fighting. Much of this was based on the techniques of guerilla warfare, developed into a new military doctrine by innovators such as Orde Wingate. His Chindit irregulars used long marches and air drops to penetrate deep behind the Japanese lines, with the aim of disrupting their communications and supplies. They used the jungle to their advantage, trying to stay away from places where the Japanese could bring tanks and heavy artillery to bear. The practical effectiveness of the Chindits was limited, whether through faults in Wingate's thinking or due to the intervention of officers who disagreed with his approach. But their bold campaigns unsettled the Japanese and boosted the morale of Allied forces in the region.

The British also worked on recruiting local forces to resist the Japanese. Special operatives went behind the lines to recruit local tribes and former Burma Rifles, ready to rise up against the Japanese when the time came. As in Europe, the Allies kept their enemies stretched thin by supporting resistance to their rule.

Japanese rule in the Pacific was particularly harsh. Brutal punishment of dissidents and captured enemy combatants was common. Thousands of Allied servicemen died in terrible conditions in prison, as did Western civilians herded into camps in occupied territories. This was not the systematic extinction that would eventually be revealed in Europe, but an imperial regime willing to use cruel tactics to achieve its aims. No nation emerged from the war with clean hands, but the Japanese earned a particularly terrible reputation among their neighbors.

Chapter 9 – Operation Torch and the Taking of North Africa

Though Japanese aggression had drawn America into immediate fighting in the Pacific, this was not the strategic priority for any of the main players in the Allied camp. Europe was their priority, and the American government was keen to get involved. American planes and pilots went to join the British in their bombardment of German cities, attacks which struck the same terror into the Germans that they had inflicted upon London and the industrial cities of England. But what the Americans really wanted was to put boots on the ground.

The American government's preferred option was to launch an invasion of mainland Europe. Churchill convinced them that this should not be their starting point. First, they would defeat the Axis in north Africa and the Mediterranean. Then they could make a move on France.

Out of this strategic decision, Operation Torch was born. This was an Anglo-American operation, with the Americans providing the bulk of the forces while the British brought their experience and knowledge of the war in North Africa.

Operation Torch began on November 8, 1942. Over 100,000 personnel made three separate seaborne landings at different points along the coast of northwest Africa, all targeted territory held by the Vichy French. The furthest east would position the Allies to threaten the Germans in Tunisia.

The Torch landings were generally a success. The French response was mixed, some resisting while others gladly went over to the Allied side. Within days, the Allies had a solid foothold in Africa.

Having established themselves, the Allies began a campaign to conquer Tunisia. The ports of Tunis and Bizerte were particularly critical, as these were the main harbors remaining to the Axis forces. Rommel and the Afrika Corps were already retreating in the face of Montgomery's troops in the east. If they could be cut off the west and deprived of their escape route then it would be a huge victory for the Allies.

The advance wasn't an easy one. Supply lines had to be arranged across hundreds of miles of Algerian desert. The first attempt to take Tunisia, by the British First Army, was repulsed by a strong German force including air support from the Luftwaffe, who had bases close to the front line.

In December, a second attempt on Tunis also met with failure. American, British, and French forces struggled to work together in difficult and unfamiliar conditions. Air support for the Allies was not as good as for the Axis forces. The advance made it as far as Longstop Hill, a high point with good views of the ground toward Tunis, and the two sides fought for the hill for four days over Christmas. But the attempt to reach Tunis failed. Then came rainy weather, turning the ground to mud, and further advances had to be postponed.

Tensions were high in the Allied armies as they sat out the winter of 1942-3. The British had more experience of war, not just from this one but from their long history as a colonial power. The Americans, on the other hand, were confident and outspoken, the representatives of a superpower on the rise. The British found the Americans boastful despite their inexperience. The Americans found the British cold and patronizing. There were bar fights between the soldiers and tense arguments among the high command.

In January 1943, Montgomery reached Tripoli. There he stopped to rest and repair before he continued his pursuit of Rommel.

Rommel took the opportunity to create a defensive position on the Mareth Line, where he believed that he could hold the British up with minimal resources. This would give him the freedom to attack the less experienced forces to the west.

On February 14, Rommel launched his attack against American forces at Sidi Bou Zid in the strategically important Faid Pass. He routed the Americans and then drove off their hastily assembled counter-attack.

From the Faid Pass, Rommel moved on to the Kasserine Pass. Here, he was held up by British forces, which fought a careful delaying action as they retreated from the German assault. Though Rommel won control of the pass, he had lost momentum, left his flank exposed, and over-extended his supply lines. The advance could not be maintained.

Instead, Rommel turned east, attacking Montgomery at Medenine. The British commander was used to his opponent's tactics and prepared a good defensive position, with British and New Zealand troops firing on the flank of Rommel's force as it advanced. The Germans were soundly defeated. Rommel was summoned home by Hitler, leaving the African troops in the hands of the more cautious Von Arnim.

Meanwhile, American morale declined. They had not yet had a significant victory and British successes were only making their allies more arrogant. Something had to change.

The first thing to go was one of the American commanders, General Fredendall, an indecisive leader whose hostility to the British had contributed to tensions among the commanders. He was replaced by General George Patton, one of the most colorful, bold, and abrasive characters of the war. Patton's new deputy was Omar

Bradley, who in a quieter way would also prove to be one of America's best commanders.

While the Germans retreated west, British officers set up training programs to better prepare American troops. It wasn't a popular move, given that it played into the image of British superiority, but it helped to toughen the men up for the coming fight.

Shortly after taking command of his part of the frontline forces, Patton launched an attack that took the airfield at Gafsa. When Von Arnim launched a counter-attack, Patton's troops again defeated the Germans at the Battle of El Guettar. It wasn't a massive engagement, but it was a symbolically important one. It proved to the British that the Americans could hold their own.

Montgomery went back on the offensive in March, launching an attack on the Mareth Line. A direct assault by the British was driven off after 24 hours of heavy fighting. But the New Zealand Corps, with support from the air and from other British troops, made a flanking maneuver that broke through the enemy lines. The Axis forces retreated ten miles then made another stand, inflicting heavy casualties on the British. At last the Germans retreated again, until they were only 50 miles from the port of Tunis.

With an eye to what would follow after Africa, the Allies tried to cut off the retreat of the Axis forces. This led to failure at Fondouk Pass for an American force under General Ryder. The result was yet more arguing among the Allies, as Patton blamed the British air support and the British air commander blamed the quality of the American troops. General Eisenhower, the American officer in overall command of the Allied forces, ended up ordering an apology out of the outraged British commander.

Divisions continued as General Alexander drew up the plan for the final campaign. It gave the lead to the British, with the Americans taking only a minor role. Under pressure from politicians back home and commanders in the field, Eisenhower persuaded Alexander to change his plan. The Americans would take Bizerte.

The attack on Bizerte provided redemption for Ryder, the embarrassed commander from Fondouk Pass. Following five days of fighting, his infantry and armor launched a combined assault that took control of the critical Hill 609. They then fought off a series of counter-attacks.

American forces also broke through the defenses of Bizerte, cutting off any Axis escape.

When Hitler refused to send more supplies, Von Arnim found himself in an impossible position. He surrendered on May 12, along with 150,000 troops.

The Allies now controlled North Africa, and with it the southern Mediterranean. Though tensions remained between the different nations, the Americans had gained vital experience and prestige. The time was fast approaching for them to do what they had wanted from the start.

The Western Allies were about to invade Europe.

Chapter 10 – The Tide Turns in Eastern Europe

On the Eastern Front, the balance of the war had shifted decisively in favor of the Soviets. Germany's best hope had always lain in a decisive strike that would cripple the USSR. In Poland and France, this had been achieved in a matter of weeks. In North Africa, the greatest successes had come not from a slow grind but from swift actions that caught the Allies off guard. But in the USSR, that swift strike had not brought the results the Germans needed. Instead of knocking out the Soviet military machine and taking key cities, the Germans had become bogged down in fighting that had now lasted over two years.

In a war of attrition, the Soviets had the edge thanks to their large population and high-volume approach to armaments production. The Germans could counter the T-34 tank with their own Tigers and Panthers, but they couldn't make as much materiel as the Soviets. Weight of numbers and Soviet tenacity had thwarted German ambitions.

In the summer of 1943, the Soviets began a counter-offensive on multiple fronts. This began with an advance on the Orel salient, where German forces had been holding out since their failure to reach Moscow during Operation Barbarossa. Further south, the Soviets broke through positions around Belgorod and advanced on Kharkov. A war of movement saw the Soviets get around the Germans' flank, forcing them to pull back. By the end of August, both Orel and Kharkov had been retaken.

Hitler at last allowed his forces to pull back to the Dnieper river. Here, the Germans had planned to build a defensive line like the fortifications on their border with France. But these fortifications had not yet been built, and so the

German forces found themselves trying to hold a position that had not been prepared.

The Soviets pressed relentlessly on. Though an attempt to get around the German lines with paratroopers failed, other forces got across the Dnieper and formed bridgeheads, forcing the Germans back. Hitler insisted that his generals cling to the Dnieper line.

A counterattack by German Panzer troops briefly held up the Soviets west of Kiev. But it wasn't enough to form a solid line. Panzer divisions were repeatedly surrounded by Soviet troops and had to make costly breakouts to avoid capture.

In the north, the Soviets made little effort to advance until January 1944. When it came, the shock of the Soviet attack sent the Germans reeling. They were driven back from Leningrad. Novgorod was retaken. The Soviets pushed toward the Baltic Sea, hoping to use it to threaten Germany's eastern territories. Soon, they were at the border of Estonia, where some locals joined up to fight for the Germans rather than suffer a second Soviet occupation.

By now, Stalin was working in cooperation with the Western Allies. Together, they decided on a massive Russian offensive in Belarus, to coincide with the Anglo-American invasion of Western Europe.

By the time the attack was launched on June 22, 1944, German troops had already been stripped from the east to man the new Western front. Massive Soviet forces faced weakened German lines and their superiority in numbers quickly brought victory. Within a month, they had reached the Polish border. By the end of August, the Germans had lost 400,000 dead, wounded, or missing, while the Russians had lost less than half that number.

In July, another offensive was launched in the south. Western Ukraine was retaken. From there, Soviet forces pressed on into Romania. A coup there replaced the Axis-oriented government, leading to peace between Russia and Romania in September.

Meanwhile, a fresh offensive was launched against Finland. Just like in the Winter War, the Soviets found the Finns tougher opponents than they had anticipated. Though they quickly broke through the first two lines of Finnish defenses, the Finns retreated, regrouped, and held them at a third line.

Though the Finns were holding off the Soviets for now, they knew that it could not last. In September, the Finns made peace with the Russians, agreeing to an armistice that included punitive payments to the victors. As part of the agreement, German troops had to be hastily evacuated from Finland, harassed by their former allies along the way. This deprived the Germans of important mineral resources that had been coming out of Finland.

As the Soviets approached Poland, local forces rose up against the Germans. The Polish Home Army, one of the largest and most organized resistance networks in Europe, launched Operation Tempest. This was a series of risings meant to coincide with the approach of Soviet troops, so that the Poles could join with them in defeating the Germans. The aim was both to drive out the Nazis and to establish an independent Polish government before the Soviets could take over.

Stalin, seeing the dual aims of Tempest, held his forces back. In the most infamous incident, a massive rising in Warsaw was put down by the Germans after Soviet troops failed to come to the aid of the Poles.

Similar events took place further south. The Slovak National Uprising, launched in August 1944, tried to overthrow the government collaborating with the Nazis in occupied Slovakia and to throw out the Germans. Though the insurgency was largely put down, it marked the beginning of a period of increased guerilla operations by the Slovaks, which continued until Allies forces reached their country in 1945.

In September 1944, the Soviets launched a series of operations along the northern stretch of the Eastern Front, known collectively as the Baltic Offensive. They drove back the German forces occupying Estonia and Lithuania. The remains of the German Army Group North were cut off from the rest of the German forces, contained in a shrinking pocket of territory on the Baltic coast. Hundreds of thousands of German soldiers and civilians were trapped, living in fear of how they would be treated when the Soviet army arrived.

There was good reason for many of them to fear. The Soviets were embittered not just by invasion and years of war but also by the murderous behavior of the German SS in occupied territories. The soldiers of the Red Army had seen how barbarously their people had been treated. The desire for revenge, stoked by Soviet propaganda, fueled hatred of the Germans.

In January 1945, the Soviets finally entered Warsaw. The city was in ruins, destroyed both by the war and by the Germans as an act of punishment for Polish resistance. Soviet forces were already pushing south from Poland into Slovakia. Now, as they headed east, they reached Germany itself.

Launched in January 1945, the Vistula-Oder offensive was a remarkable achievement. Outnumbering the Germans they faced by five or six to one, the Soviets punched their way east, sometimes advancing over twenty miles in a day. They took control of the remaining Baltic states and East Prussia. Along the way, they suffered 194,000 casualties. When the operation was called to a halt in February, they were on the River Oder, less than 50 miles from Berlin.

By early 1945, the German armed forces were in ruins across Eastern Europe. From his hidden command bunkers, Hitler sent out orders for the reorganization of armies, for counter-offensives, for defensive lines to be held. But Axis resources were stretched thin, as the Allies made advances on other fronts. Around the world, the war had shifted against Hitler and his allies.

Chapter 11 – Advancing on Japan

A critical change in the tide of war in the Pacific was also seen in 1943. In the early stages, the Japanese had steadily advanced down the long chain of islands separating the Pacific from the Indian Ocean. Now the flow was reversed. Having halted the Japanese at Guadalcanal, the Allies began driving them north.

One of the first offensive operations happened further out into the Pacific, in the Gilbert Islands. There, the American Admiral Nimitz launched a seaborne invasion in November 1943. Makin was easily captured but Tarawa proved more challenging. One thousand US Marines were killed and another 2,100 wounded taking a tiny cluster of islands from the Japanese. The losses shocked the American public, but in the long term the problems faced at Tarawa saved lives. They taught vital lessons about how to carry out an amphibious assault, lessons which would be applied in the invasion of Normandy the following summer.

Next to fall were the Marshall Islands. Here, the Japanese dug in in an attempt to tie up Allied troops and supply chains. Heavy bombardments by American ships softened up Japanese positions ready for the attacks, providing Allied troops with easier landings when they arrived in January 1944. The Japanese base at Truk in the Carolines came under particularly heavy bombardment to keep it from supporting the Japanese elsewhere.

In June, the Allies began invading the Marianas. The invasion of Saipan set the tone for this fighting, as the Japanese dug in, using caves and bunkers to protect them from the American bombardment. Troops had to take them out one strongpoint at a time, an exhausting business that strained men's morale and cost heavy casualties. The same tactics would be repeated as the Japanese clung to their conquests all the way up the western Pacific. At every stage, the Allies became bogged down dealing with smaller and smaller pockets of resistance.

While the battle for Saipan was still raging, Admiral Jisaburo Ozawa tried to counter American advances. On June 19, he attacked the American 5th Fleet in the Battle of the Philippine Sea. Ozawa had nine aircraft carriers to the Americans' fifteen and was relying on support from land-based aircraft. But those planes had already been put out of action by Allied raids. The Americans destroyed the waves of Japanese planes sent against them. Their submarines and bombers destroyed many of the Japanese carriers. The Japanese withdrew with heavy losses.

In the skies, the Allies now dominated. They had a huge advantage in aircraft carriers. Their planes, though not always as agile as the Japanese fighters, were generally sturdier. With the fall of Saipan, they were able to establish an air base within bomber range of the Japanese mainland.

On November 12, 1944, a flight of 100 bombers set out on the first air raid against Tokyo since the symbolic Doolittle Raid of 1942. This time, the bombers meant business. Over the months that followed, bombs would devastate Japanese cities, bringing the sort of ruin previously seen in Europe.

The value of such bombing has been seriously questioned since the war. In Britain in particular, Bomber Command clung to the tactics of terror bombing, aiming to smash enemy industry and morale. This was done despite the evidence about its effectiveness, not because of it. But the ability of the Americans to strike at Japan certainly unsettled the government there. Following the fall of Saipan, the entire cabinet resigned. To many in government, defeat looked increasingly inevitable.

In July 1944, US Marines invaded the island of Guam, the first American territory seized by the Japanese in 1941. Despite fierce Japanese counter-attacks, they took the island through a month of hard fighting. Only ten miles long and thirty miles wide, Guam cost the Americans 1,440 men dead, 145 missing, and 5,648 wounded; 10,693 Japanese died. When the island fell, many of the rest fled into the jungle to fight on. One of them did not emerge until 1972.

Tinian, the last significant part of the Marianas, fell more easily. A surprise attack by US Marines from Saipan established a beachhead on the island. Within a week, they had taken out the entire Japanese garrison.

The desperate fighting of the Japanese unsettled the Americans. But the real cost of such tactics fell upon Japan. In the fighting for the Marianas, they lost almost ten times as many men dead or captured as their enemies were killed.

The next stop in the American advance was a symbolically important one—the Philippines. The Philippines had been held by American forces when the Japanese invaded in 1941. Thousands of American servicemen had been taken prisoner when the islands fell. General MacArthur, who had been in charge of defending the Philippines, was now in charge of American forces fighting in the Pacific and was determined to make good his promise to return to the islands.

The Americans began their invasion of the Philippines in October 1944, when troops landed on Leyte and nearby islands. The Japanese responded by launching a plan named Sho-Go or Operation Victory. This was the last great effort by the Japanese navy to keep the American threat away from their homeland and to protect the oil supplies that would keep the fleet in action. To do this, they sent naval forces toward Leyte in three separate groups, with the aim of hitting the Allied invasion force with heavy air attacks. But American and Australian fleets encountered the Japanese ships as they came into the Leyte Gulf and picked them off in separate pieces. It was one of the largest naval engagements in history and a disaster for the Japanese. They lost four aircraft carriers and 24 other fighting ships, while their opponents lost one light carrier and five other vessels.

The Gulf of Leyte was the first time the Japanese made concerted use of a new form of warfare—kamikaze attacks. Pilots flying planes loaded with explosives and fuel made suicide attacks on Allied ships, using their planes as massive munitions. Such desperate tactics became a regular feature of the war from then on, young men sacrificing their lives piloting kamikaze boats and planes in defense of the homeland.

In January, the Allies landed on Luzon, the most important of the Philippine islands. With the Japanese fleet so badly mauled, there was little prospect of support or rescue for the Japanese troops there. They fought on not in hopes of victory but with the intention of holding up the enemy for as long as possible. When the city of Manila fell at the end of January, troops took to the hills, where they fought on until June.

On the Asian mainland, the Japanese spent the first half of 1944 on the offensive, with attacks in China and India.

The attack on British-controlled India came first. Following a diversionary attack in February, the main offensive began in early March. But the diversion was defeated too quickly, freeing up British and Indian forces to tackle the main thrust. The Japanese were halted and then driven back at Imphal and Kohima. Supply lines failed and disease began to take its toll. By June, the Japanese forces were in retreat, many soldiers refusing to obey orders for a counter-attack. At the start of July, the offensive was called off.

Operation Ichi-Go, the offensive against China, was more of a success. The Chinese forces were not as well trained, led, or organized as those of their allies, despite support and training from the British and Americans. Over the course of eight months, the Japanese significantly increased their holdings in China. The aim was not just to take territory from the Chinese, but also to deprive the Americans of airfields in China from which they were bombing the Japanese. In this regard, it was a limited success as there was disruption but the Americans found other bases of operations. In taking territory, it was something of a self-defeating victory. The Japanese took control of cities but could not control the countryside around them. Their troops ended up spread thin to govern what they had taken. And while it was a significant blow for the Chinese nationalists under Chiang Kai-Shek, it did little to impede the advance of the Western Allies.

The defeat of the Japanese invasion of India opened the way for fresh Allied attacks into Burma. They drove back the broken Japanese forces then followed them into the occupied territory in late 1944.

Early in 1945, the Allies began a series of amphibious landings. Targeting territory further south in Burma, they took control of islands and peninsulas, inflicting a series of defeats and some heavy casualties on the Japanese. In the north, ongoing offensives achieved progress despite the withdrawal of some Chinese troops to counter the Ichi-Go offensive.

By early 1945, the Japanese were being pushed back everywhere except mainland China. For them, the war was not yet lost, but there was no visible way that it could be won.

Chapter 12 – The Invasion of Italy

Though Germany and Japan were both under pressure from the middle of 1943, neither was the first part of the Axis to give way. That honor would go to the oldest of Europe's far right regimes and the weak link in the chain of Hitler's ambitions—Fascist Italy.

With Africa taken, Churchill proposed that the Anglo-American forces there move on to attack the "soft underbelly" of Axis Europe. The Italians had shown in both Africa and the Balkans that they were not as formidable militarily as their German comrades. A landing in Italy was likely to be easier than almost anywhere else in Europe, despite the presence of German forces sent to reinforce the Italians. Supply routes could be maintained thanks to Allied control of Malta and North Africa. And from Italy, the Allies could march north into the heart of Hitler's empire.

The American focus was still on a direct assault into northern Europe. But the British persuaded them to accept a compromise strategy. A smaller invasion of Italy in 1943 would keep the Mediterranean war going, while the bulk of Allied forces prepared to invade France the following year.

The first step in the invasion of Italy was to take the island of Sicily. This began on July 10, 1943, when paratroopers and seaborne forces landed on the island. It was a joint Anglo-American operation, with the Americans led by Patton and the British by Montgomery. The two men's dislike of each other fueled a rivalry that helped to drive them on but did little for cooperation between the Allies.

The main advance toward Messina was meant to be made by the British. When they were held up by Italian and German troops, Patton took the opportunity to increase the

Americans' role. Through advances north and then east, he reached Messina before the British.

The Axis forces evacuated the island, leaving it in Allied hands in the middle of August. The fighting had lasted just over a month, during which time the Allies had gained further valuable experience of amphibious and airborne assaults.

Meanwhile, Mussolini's political position was crumbling beneath his feet. Seeing that an Allied invasion of Italy was likely, he had begged Hitler to make peace with the USSR and send his troops west to face the threat. Hitler refused.

The invasion of Sicily further undermined Mussolini's position. Hitler summoned him to a humiliating meeting on July 19. On the same day, an Allied bombing raid hit Rome for the first time, highlighting Italy's newfound vulnerability.

Within the Italian leadership, Mussolini's friends were turning against him. His Fascist colleagues called upon King Victor Emmanuel III to retake the constitutional powers that had been taken by Mussolini. On July 25, the king replaced Mussolini with Marshal Badoglio and had the former dictator arrested.

When this news got out, many Italians celebrated, believing that the war was over. But it wouldn't be that easy. Badoglio maintained the pretense of loyalty to Germany, even as he negotiated a peace with the Allies. Despite his protests, German troops moved into the country, ready to deal with a potential Italian defection. An armistice agreement with the Allies was signed by Badoglio's representatives on September 3 but kept secret for several days.

On the same day that the armistice was signed, Allied troops crossed the Strait of Messina and landed in mainland Italy. They faced little opposition. The Italians were in disarray, many unopposed to the arrival of the British and Americans. The Germans correctly believed that this was not the main invasion force and so held back.

On September 8, the armistice signed by Badoglio's government was made public. Italy was surrendering to the Allies. The Germans had been preparing for this possibility. Within minutes of the official announcement, they launched Operation Achse. Italian troops across Europe were contained and disarmed by the Germans. In Italy, the Germans seized control of the north of the country, effectively turning it into another occupied territory. In the south, forces commanded by Kesselring continued their tactics of slow retreat and resistance to the Allies.

On the 9th, the Allies launched their main invasion. At Taranto, British troops landed with relatively little difficulty. At Salerno, the Americans faced stiff opposition from the Germans, who at first managed to contain them within a limited beachhead on the coast. But German efforts were hampered by the need to manage the Italians. The Allied troops, many of them veterans of the North African campaign, began to advance up the peninsula.

Meanwhile, Hitler was making moves to keep political control of Italy. Schemes were hatched to kidnap the king and government, but these came to nothing. The one success came in the rescue of Mussolini. The former dictator was due to be handed over to the Allies as part of Italy's surrender, and he was being moved around to keep him out of German hands. But on September 12, a daring raid by German commandos took him out of Italian hands and into those of the Nazis.

To call it a rescue would be to overstate Mussolini's degree of freedom after the raid. He went from being a captive of his fellow countrymen to a relatively comfortable captive of the Germans. He was used as a puppet leader for the Italian Social Republic, as the

Germans had labeled the part of Italy they occupied. He was a symbol that allowed them to add legitimacy to that occupation.

As the Allies advanced toward Rome, they faced an increasingly difficult campaign. Mountainous terrain divided by rivers made for a challenging advance. Field Marshal Kesselring had convinced Hitler that the Germans should defend southern Italy, keeping Allied air power as far from Germany as possible for as long as possible. This also bought time to prepare defensive lines further north.

A German defensive line south of Rome held the Allies up for months over the winter of 1943-4. American, British, Canadian, French, and Polish troops were all brought into action in a series of offensives aimed at breaking through a narrow part of the front close to Monte Cassino. At last, in May 1944, they did it. An opportunity was missed to trap the German 10th Army as it retreated, but the symbolically important city of Rome was occupied without a fight on June 4.

The Allied invasion of France a few days later led to a change in the Allied forces in Italy. Experienced units were withdrawn ready for operations to take southern France. Other troops were sent to replace them, including some from Brazil, which had joined the Allied side in 1942. But these could not entirely make up for the loss of veteran soldiers.

In August 1944, the Allies began another substantial offensive in Italy. They made progress, but not as much as Churchill wanted. This was not the decisive victory he sought, one which would let them get into Eastern Europe before the Soviets and help set the stage for the new post-war order.

Partisan activity was on the rise. Resistance groups, many of them motivated by left-wing politics, took up arms against the Germans in the north and in the border region between Allied and Axis Italy. As other Italians fought on for the Germans, the fight for Italy took on an element of civil war.

By early 1945, winter weather, combined with the need to withdraw troops to other fronts, brought the Allied advance to a temporary halt. Italy lay divided, as did the attention of the Western Allies. The eyes of the world were now on France.

Chapter 13 – From D-Day to the Bulge

While it is unfair on the soldiers who fought in Italy that their campaign is not better remembered, it is also unsurprising. It was overshadowed by another operation carried out by the Western Allies, one so bold and so ingenious that it remains one of the most amazing accomplishments in the history of warfare.

This was Operation Overlord.

The Germans were expecting the Allied invasion of Western Europe to come through northern France. It was a logical option, given the short distance across the Channel from England. They therefore prepared for such an invasion, building up the defensive system known as the Atlantic Wall. Obstacles were placed on beaches. Concrete fortifications were built all along the coast. Artillery was put into place and troops stationed to repel the attack.

The Allies made extensive preparations of their own. From July 1943 onwards, they began training and practicing for the invasion, which would consist of an amphibious assault combined with airborne landings and supported by bombardments by sea and air. Massive floating components for harbors were constructed, so that they could follow the troops across the Channel and allow supplies to be unloaded. These Mulberry harbors meant that the Allies didn't have to start by seizing a port.

The Allies also began a massive campaign of deception to trick the Germans into expecting the main attack to come around the French port of Calais. The German agents the British had turned at the start of the war fed misinformation to their handlers. The First US Army Group was created, a non-existent force supposedly based in south-east England. Set and prop makers from the theaters of London were brought out to mock up an army camp, radio signals were sent out just to be intercepted, and General Patton, taken out of real command for mistreatment of soldiers in Italy, was put in charge to convince the Germans that the army was a real threat.

The invasion was launched on June 6, 1944. The night before, signals went out to the French resistance to sabotage German communication and transport systems. Just after midnight, 24,000 paratroopers were dropped. As dawn approached, an armada sailed across the Channel from England.

It was the largest amphibious invasion in history. Over 4,000 ships, barges, and landing craft were used to deposit 133,000 soldiers onto five stretches of the Norman coast. Two of the beaches were taken by the Americans, two by the British, and one by the Canadians.

These landings took place in the face of German forces and many men died before even making it off the beaches. Casualties were at their highest for the Americans on Omaha Beach, where they became trapped beneath high cliffs.

Months of preparation paid off. Though the Allies didn't take their objectives on the first day, they all managed to establish holds on the French coast. While Hitler held back forces to face the invasion he still expected at Calais, the Allies began fighting their way inland.

On June 12, the Allies linked up their five bridgeheads. They held a stretch of land 60 miles long and up to 15 miles in depth, but major objectives, including the town of Caen, remained in German hands.

The problem for the Allies was the Norman countryside. With its narrow, winding roads between tall hedgerows, it gave the advantage to the defenders, who had plenty of places to lie in ambush. The Allies also struggled to overcome stiff German resistance in key places. It took until July 21 to completely take Caen, by which time the town was in ruins.

On the other hand, troops and supplies were pouring in. The Mulberry harbors were a success. Though one was destroyed in a storm on June 19, the other was repaired and remained operational. Over the next ten months, it would be used to unload 2.5 million men and 4 million tons of supplies.

Among the German high command, there was a growing realization that the war could not be won and that Hitler could not be reasoned with. On July 20, a group of German officers and politicians tried to assassinate him with a bomb, so that they could take over and make peace with the Allies. They failed. Hitler purged the upper echelons of the German army. Rommel, the hero of Africa, was among those who took their own lives rather than face trial and execution.

The Allies were making advances, but the Germans still had them contained in north-west France. A breakthrough was needed.

That breakthrough came with Operation Cobra. Launched on July 25, this was a concerted effort by the Americans to apply huge pressure against the Germans in a single sector. Once the enemy lines had been weakened, the US Third Army, led by a reinstated Patton, punched through and headed out across France.

This was the Allies turning the German's own tactics against them, a fast-moving column of armored troops creating a hole in the enemy lines, then launching an aggressive campaign that left the defenders without time to recover. It was an attack of which Guderian or Rommel would have been proud.

Between Patton's breakthrough and advances elsewhere along the lines, a substantial portion of the German forces became surrounded at Falaise. The Germans rushed to get out of the trap while the Allies hurried to complete their encirclement. Though many Germans escaped, 50,000 were captured.

Falaise showed that the rifts at the top of the Allied hierarchy were still not healed, as Patton blamed Montgomery for the failure to close the gap sooner and so capture more Germans.

Patton's breakout and the fall of the Falaise pocket signaled the end of any hopes the Axis forces had of containing the Allies. Allied troops made broad advances across France, while their opponents, ordered to hold every inch of ground by Hitler, were forced into a fighting retreat.

In Germany, hasty preparations were being made to defend the homeland. The Siegfried Line, a system of defenses along the border with France, had been abandoned as unnecessary in 1940. Now, rusted padlocks were removed from bunkers and empty stores were resupplied as troops arrived. Attacking the Siegfried Line would cost the Allies dearly in blood and time, but like the Maginot Line before it, it would not be enough to hold back invasion.

In Paris, the French Resistance rose up against the Germans on August 19. American and French troops rushed to aid the city as the Germans threatened to destroy it. They arrived on the 24th and on the 25th the French capital was liberated. It was a moment of huge symbolic importance, but the war for France was still ongoing.

On September 17, Allied forces under Montgomery made a bold attempt to smash through German positions in the Netherlands and strike into Germany. Operation Market Garden involved paratroop landings at a string of bridges that led deep into enemy-held territory. A swift armored advance would then break through the German lines and link up with the paratroopers, creating a route for Allied forces to outflank the Germans and cross the Rhine into

Germany.

Market Garden was an over-ambitious failure. The advance could not reach the paratroopers quickly enough. Those at the end of the line of advance were left isolated for days, fending off German attacks. They eventually had to withdraw.

The failure of Market Garden added to tensions within the Allied high command. But the Allies, unlike the Germans, had the ability to productively discuss differences, vent some of their frustrations, and let dissenting voices be heard. On the Axis side, the autocratic Hitler was unwilling to listen to those who disagreed with him, men who often understood military matters better than he did. Disagreements were suppressed and men walked on eggshells around their leader.

On December 16, Hitler launched a counter-attack. Once again moving through the relatively undefended Ardennes forest, Panzer forces aimed to break through the Allied lines at a weak point. To support this, German commandos infiltrated the Allied forces, disguising themselves as officers so that they could spread confusion among the troops. German paratroops landed behind the Allied lines so that, as in the Market Garden plan, they could hold key positions along the route to aid the advance of tanks and infantry.

This second Ardennes offensive seemed to start well. The Allies were caught by surprise and the Germans made substantial advances.

But the possibility of success was illusory. The Germans had far fewer tanks and soldiers available than in 1940, while the Allies had more men with more experience. The infiltration work had little impact, the German agents being quickly caught. As the advance slowed and then ground to a halt, the paratroopers were left isolated behind enemy lines, forced to scatter and in many cases surrender.

The failed offensive became the Battle of the Bulge, as it created a bulge in the Allied lines but not a breakthrough. The Allied advance on Germany was delayed by over a month. But that month had cost Hitler his last substantial reserves. He would never again be able to launch a counter-attack.

There was no stopping the Allied advance.

Chapter 14 – The Fall of Germany

By the beginning of 1945, Germany effectively stood alone in Europe. Though German troops still occupied large chunks of several countries, Germany's principle ally, Italy, was at war with itself. Units from other countries, including anti-Soviet partisans from various parts of Eastern Europe, still fought on the Axis side, but they all did so under German military leadership.

In the west, the Allies made steady advances into Germany itself. The British and Canadians led the charge in the north, while in the south the Americans bore the brunt of the fighting. There, the focus was on demolishing Germany's industrial might in the Ruhr region. The fall of industrial cities such as Metz deprived the Germans of the ability to produce the materials of war.

Even during the last year of the war, the Germans were proving how advanced their military technology was. Following the D-Day landings, V-1 and V-2 rockets had been launched against British cities. German jet planes joined propeller-driven aircraft in the skies above Germany, though such superior technology, deployed in small numbers, was insignificant in the overall balance of the war.

As they advanced, there were again divisions behind the scenes between the Western Allies. Churchill was eager to push forward as far as possible, to occupy land before the Soviets could, as he believed that they would not let go of any territory they took. Eisenhower was more cautious, concerned with the possibility of over-stretching in the face of the Germans. In particular, he was wary of rumors of the German Alpine Redoubt.

The Alpine Redoubt was one of two important rumors floating around the German military at the time, both untrue but both important in shaping the final months of the war.

The Alpine Redoubt was a supposed plan for German troops to set up a fortified zone in the Alps. This would become a last place of resistance, where they could hold out for a long time against the Allies. In reality, such a plan had been rejected by Hitler earlier in the war, and by the time he considered the possibility it was too late. There was no redoubt.

The other rumor, encouraged by German propagandists, was that the sides were about to change. Many Germans believed, as Churchill did, that a confrontation between the Soviets and the west was inevitable. Some believed that it would come when the Allied forces of east and west met in Germany. At that point, the more optimistic German commanders insisted, the Allies would stop fighting the remaining Germans and side with them against the menace of communism. Some German commanders tried to reach out to the Allies and make this a reality. But for all the concerns about Stalin in the west, even Churchill never considered such a plan. His priority, and that of all the Allied commanders, was putting down the German menace once and for all.

On the Eastern Front, the Soviets continued to advance through territories occupied by the Germans. They took Silesia and Pomerania and advanced into Austria, taking Vienna. In the Balkans, the Yugoslav communist resistance under Tito had become a force to be reckoned with. German troops in Yugoslavia and the locals who had sided with them looked increasingly isolated and vulnerable.

In Italy, the Allies launched their last major offensive in April 1945. As the Allied troops advanced, Italian partisans declared a general uprising. The war became a swirling mess of movement. German troops fought rearguard actions, buying time for others to retreat. In places, Allied forces got behind them, cutting off their routes of retreat.

Meanwhile, secret negotiations were underway between representatives of the German and Allied commanders in Italy. Despite Hitler's orders, the Germans were looking for a peaceful way out. These negotiations faltered at times, as the military and political situation changed, but they laid the groundwork for the end of the fighting.

Among those fleeing the battlefront was Mussolini. On April 27, his convoy was captured by partisans near Lake Como. He, his mistress, and several members of his cabinet were taken into captivity. The next day, they were shot. In an act of degradation meant as vengeance for the treatment of partisans, their bodies were strung up in Milan, where people mocked and abused the corpses. In Italy, as elsewhere in Europe, many people were bitter at the way they had been treated by Axis regimes. As the Axis fell, that bitterness spilled out.

In Germany, Hitler took desperate measures to defend his crumbling empire. Youths, old men, and those previously excluded on health grounds were called up for military service. There was little time to train or prepare them. They were given weapons and thrust into the lines, ready to fight off the advancing Allies.

Civil society was shut down to provide personnel for the military. The only parts of universities still teaching were the medical schools. Only textbooks and Hitler's books were published. Theatres and music halls closed. Even military personnel saw their lives changed, as men were stripped from the navy to bolster the army. There was no point continuing the fight at sea if the homeland was lost.

On the Eastern Front, the forces pinned against the Baltic were finally forced to surrender in the face of overwhelming Soviet might. Meanwhile, senior Nazi officials were fleeing west, often taking their close associates and wealth with them.

Earlier in the war, Hitler had moved between a number of custom-built bases around Europe. Now he hunkered down in a bunker beneath Berlin, the capital of the empire that he had thought would last for a thousand years. His behavior was increasingly erratic, his view of the situation increasingly detached from reality. He could not conceive of the possibility that Germany might lose the war. Military units were reorganized and renamed in a desperate attempt to maintain the illusion of a potent fighting force. Command positions were reshuffled as men disappointed him through their failures or through disagreeing with his views. One of his few sensible decisions was giving Kesselring independent authority in the south if the German empire should be split in two.

The Soviets were the first to reach Berlin. On April 16, they began their assault on the city. For political reasons, Stalin let two different field marshals, each with their own army and their own plan, attack the German capital.

The fighting for Berlin was as bitter as any in the war. The Germans clung on with the desperation of the lost. Some hoped to hold off the Soviets long enough for the British and Americans to arrive, saving them from the feared Red Army. Others were so thoroughly indoctrinated with Nazi ideas that they could not consider the possibility of defeat. They fought street by street, combat sometimes breaking out next to the bread lines where starving civilians queued for food.

On April 30, Soviet troops stormed the Reichstag, the official seat of German government, and flew their red victory flag above the building. It was a powerful symbolic moment, marking the ascendancy of the Soviets in the east. But on the same day, a far more important event took place in the bunker.

Hitler had reached the end of the road. Seeing that he could not win, he committed suicide alongside his wife. Rather than have his body suffer the same indignities as Mussolini's corpse, he ordered that it be burnt outside the bunker. Petrol was in short supply, but his remaining subordinates did their best, cremating their leader in the pauses between the shellfire being rained down by Soviet artillery.

With Hitler gone, surrender became an option. Forces in Italy had already surrendered on the 29th. On May 7, Germany signed an unconditional surrender to the Allies. Troops in Prague fought on against the Soviets until the 11th and many elsewhere fled to western areas before surrendering.

The battle for Europe was over, but the war raged on.

Chapter 15 – The Fall of Japan

With the Japanese in retreat, the Allies began looking ahead to the invasion of Japan. As part of their preparations, they launched increasingly intense bombing campaigns against the Japanese mainland.

The problem for these bombers was the distance involved—a round trip of 3,000 miles from Saipan to the Japanese targets. A closer base would let them carry out more raids and there was a natural choice for that base. Iwo Jima, an island 760 miles from southeast Japan, was currently a base for Japanese fighters and the radar directing them against incoming attacks. Taking it would deprive the Japanese of an important defensive position as well as bringing Allied air power forward.

After days of bombardment, US troops landed on Iwo Jima in mid-February 1945. As on many of the Japanese-occupied islands, they made the landing relatively easily but became tied down in the face of protracted Japanese resistance. It took over a month to clear the island, during which time the Americans took heavy casualties and created one of the most iconic images of the war, a photograph of the raising of the stars and stripes over Mount Suribachi.

While the Marines fought for Iwo Jima, the US Air Force was changing its approach to bombing. On March 9, they switched from daytime high-altitude raids to nighttime firebombing, using napalm against Japanese cities made largely out of wood. In that first raid, 25% of Tokyo was destroyed and 80,000 people died. Based on these results, the planners concluded that they might be able to beat Japan without risking an invasion. Firebombing was extended to other major cities, burning the urban heart out of Japan.

Though the Allies were moving away from a focus on invading Japan, they still planned for it. The next step in the island-hopping approach was Okinawa. It had a garrison of 120,000 men, 10,000 aircraft, and a naval task force including the largest battleship ever built, the *Yamato*. This would be a hard fight.

Months of air raids and weeks of naval bombardment softened up Okinawa ready for the invasion. On April 1, the Americans made an unopposed landing on the island. This was followed by another grueling campaign to take out the dug-in defenders, which lasted until the end of June. During that time, hundreds of kamikaze pilots attacked the Allied fleet, sinking over a dozen destroyers. But the Japanese fleet also suffered, with the *Yamato* among the vessels sunk by American bombers.

While the Americans fought for Okinawa, the Australians were retaking Borneo. It was an equally protracted campaign that ended at the start of July with the collapse of Japanese defenses at Balikpapan.

In Burma, the Allies continued their offensive. The focus was on taking Rangoon, to gain control of this vital port and so ensure supply lines before the monsoon rains began. As Burmese forces rebelled against the Japanese, the Allies rushed forward by land and then launched a seaborne operation. They managed to take vital positions at Rangoon hours before the monsoon rains began.

The Japanese retreated through Burma. Their attempts at a counter-attack were thwarted and they lost thousands of men trying to break out of the country.

The Allied victory in Burma helped to secure the Ledo Road, a vital supply route for the Chinese. As well as taking part in operations in Burma, Chinese Nationalist armies launched spring offensives to retake large portions of their own land, including Hunan and Guangxi. The Chinese army, aided by the Allies, was better armed and trained than at any previous point in the war. While the country was still riven by internal strife, it had gained the ability to effectively fight back, especially now that Japanese resources were being drained by the island war.

On every front, the Japanese were in retreat. A strict code of honor kept military men from accepting defeat, but that result was now inevitable. With Allied submarines preventing imports and bombers destroying cities, the country was being worn away and victory was impossible.

As in Germany a few months earlier, all that was left to be decided was the terms on which defeat took place. In July, following a meeting at Potsdam, the Allies demanded that the Japanese surrender unconditionally. The Japanese government refused.

Following the fall of Okinawa and the destruction of the Japanese fleet there, the route to the mainland lay open. With the war in Europe over, troops from there started heading to the Pacific, ready to form an army of invasion. But experience showed that this was likely to be a costly and protracted campaign, one that could cost hundreds of thousands of Allied lives.

Unknown to the world, the Allies had a trump card up their sleeve. Since 1942, American, British, and Canadian scientists had been working in secret on a new weapon. Under the code-name of the Manhattan Project, they had developed the first atomic bombs, weapons unparalleled in their devastating power.

Rather than lose lives invading Japan, President Truman chose to use this weapon to intimidate the enemy into surrender. On August 6, 1945, an atomic bomb was used for the first time. Dropped on the city of Hiroshima, this single bomb killed 70-80,000 people. Three days later, another bomb was dropped on Nagasaki, killing 35-40,000.

As many people were being killed by conventional bombs, but the devastating power of the atom bomb shook the world. As unsettling for the Japanese was a declaration of war by the Soviets, who invaded the Japanese puppet state of Manchuria on August 9. Despite the wider war, the USSR had not previously been fighting Japan. Now there was no hope that the Soviets would act as a moderating force for the Japanese in negotiations with the Allies.

On September 2, the Japanese surrendered unconditionally to General MacArthur on the USS *Missouri*.

The Second World War was over. The question now was what its consequences would be.

Chapter 16 – Aftermath

In Europe, a fresh war threatened to break out immediately, as Tito's Yugoslav forces tried to occupy parts of Austria. Swift maneuvers by the Western Allies cut off these ambitions, but there were concerns that Stalin might back Tito, giving him the confidence to fight. Fortunately, Stalin wasn't interested in supporting Yugoslav ambition. Tito's plans came to nothing.

Tito's behavior threatened to plunge the world back into war. But other revelations transformed people's understanding of the war and of what it meant to be human.

As Allied troops advanced across Europe, they discovered the Nazi concentration camps. Unknown to most people, Hitler's regime had been murdering Jews, gays, Slavs, dissidents, and others they saw as opponents. This wasn't just an occasional killing. It was the systematic murder of millions of innocent people, using buildings and machines designed just for this purpose.

It was the most horrifying act ever committed by humanity. The revelation of the torments inflicted in Japanese prison camps only added to a sense of collective horror. Entire fields of social psychology developed just to understand how this could happen. The international Jewish community, devastated by their losses, gained a renewed determination to found a safe, secure homeland of their own.

War crimes trials followed. The world came together in condemnation not only of the camps but of other murders carried out during the war. Senior Nazi officials were tried at Nuremberg. Ten men were hanged. One committed suicide to escape execution. Many more were imprisoned.

The process of recovery was about more than retribution. The Allies carried out a thorough program to remove Nazi influences from Germany and to help the country rebuild, so as not to leave an embittered nation seeking revenge, as it had after World War One. The United Nations was founded to create a place for nations to peacefully settle their differences, and so to avoid another war.

While the World War was over, the Cold War was just beginning. Churchill and a throng of senior Germans had been right—confrontation between the Soviet Union and the capitalist west was now inevitable. The question was how it would play out.

In the aftermath of the war, Europe was divided into two spheres of influence. In the east, the Soviets spread communist rule. In the west, the Americans, British, and French ensured the ascendancy of capitalist democracy. For decades, the two faced off against each other. The fear of global war and of atomic weapons, as demonstrated during the Second World War, kept them from direct conflict, even as they fought through proxy nations.

Outside of Europe, the Second World War marked the effective end of Europe's overseas empires. The Italians and Germans lost their colonies in the war. The British, Dutch, and French were left in no condition to reclaim those they had lost or to retain those now yearning for freedom. Over the following twenty years, their former colonies broke free, some peacefully and some by force.

Into their place stepped the USA, the ascendant global power. Having cast off isolationism and proved their power, the Americans were determined to use it. They became the leaders of the Western world, politically as well as economically. The Second World War had turned an introverted nation into a global powerhouse.

Conclusion

The Second World War was the most devastating conflict that the Earth had ever seen. To say that all the world took part would be an exaggeration. After all, much of Africa and nearly all of Latin America stayed out of the conflict. Even several European countries did not fight. But it was a conflict of such scale that the whole world was transformed.

The effects of the war linger to this day, from the horrifying memories of the prison camps to the unifying impact of the United Nations. As the generation that fought the war passes away, it is more important than ever that we remember what happened and why, so that such devastation should never happen again.

If you enjoyed this book, then I'd really appreciate it if you would post a short review on Amazon. I read all the reviews myself so that I can continue to provide books that people want.

Thanks for your support!

**Check out another book by
Captivating History**

Make sure to check out more books from Captivating History

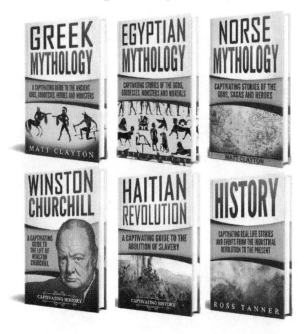

Free Bonus from Captivating History: History Ebook (Available for a Limited time)

Hi History Lovers!

Now you have a chance to join our exclusive history list so you can get your first history ebook for free as well as discounts and a potential to get more history books for free! Simply visit the link below to join.

Captivatinghistory.com/ebook

Also, make sure to follow us on:

Twitter: @Captivhistory

Facebook: Captivating History: @captivatinghistory

Bibliography

Hugh Ambrose (2010), *The Pacific.*

Jim Baggott (2009), *Atomic: The First War of Physics and the Secret History of the Atom Bomb, 1939-49.*

Ralph Bennett (1999), *Behind the Battle: Intelligence in the War with Germany 1939-1945.*

Nigel Cawthorne (2004), *Turning the Tide: Decisive Battles of the Second World War.*

Francis Crosby (2010), *The Complete Guide to Fighters & Bombers of the World.*

John Ellis (1993), *The World War II Databook.*

Ian V. Hogg and John Weeks (1980), *The Illustrated Encyclopedia of Military Vehicles.*

Richard Holmes, ed. (2001), *The Oxford Companion to Military History.*

John Keegan (1987), *The Mask of Command.*

Orr Kelly (2002), *Meeting the Fox: The Allied Invasion of Africa, from Operation Torch to Kasserine Pass to Victory in Tunisia.*

James Lucas (1986), *Last Days of the Reich.*

James Lucas (1996), *Hitler's Enforcers: Leaders of the German War Machine 1939-1945.*

David Rooney (1999), *Military Mavericks: Extraordinary Men of Battle.*

Conrad Totman (2005), *A History of Japan*, second edition.

Charles Whiting (1999), *West Wall: The Battle for Hitler's Siegfried Line.*

Made in United States
Troutdale, OR
10/05/2023

13436279R00051